When Your Cup is Empty

How to Refill Yourself with Self-Care and Self-Love

Empowerment Workable Journal

When Your Cup is Empty

How to Refill Yourself with Self-Care and Self-Love
Empowerment Workable Journal

Adrienne K. Thomas

Copyright © 2022, When Your Cup is Empty, How to Refill Yourself with Self-Care and Self-Love, Adrienne K. Thomas

ISBN: 979-8588762182

All rights reserved. This book or any portion thereof may not be reproduced or used in any manner whatsoever without the express written permission of the publisher except for the use of brief quotations in a book review.

Formatted and edited by
Written Word Editorial
www.sheliawritesbooks.com

TABLE OF CONTENTS

INTRODUCTION	i
GAINING THROUGH LOSING	iv
WHAT IS YOUR IDEA OF SELF-CARE?	1
WHY IS SELF-CARE IMPORTANT TO YOU?	2
THE AREAS OF SELF-CARE	3
WHO AM I?	8
YOUR SELF-WORTH	12
SELF-CARE MENU	14
HOW DOES LOVE DEFINE YOU?	15
GRATEFUL	16
BROKEN	20
FAILURE	21
A SPECIAL WORD ABOUT MOTHERS	22
DO NOT BE AFRAID TO ASK FOR HELP	23
FORGIVE	24
ARE YOU AN OVERCOMER?	26
MY FUTURE	29
HEALTHY RELATIONSHIP CHECKLIST	31
SELF-CARE ACTIVITIES	32
VISION BOARD ACTIVITY	33
MY VISION BOARD	35
VISION BOARD ACTIVITY QUESTIONAIRE	37
SMALL STEPS TOWARDS A MORE POSITIVE APPROACH	38
PUZZLE #1	38
PUZZLE #2	39
WHO IS THAT IN THE MIRROR?	40
MONTHLY SELF-CARE ACTIVITY CALENDAR	41
SELF-CARE CALENDAR 1	42
SELF-CARE CALENDAR 2	43
SELF-CARE CALENDAR 3	44
HAVE FUN – COLOR ME	45
LOVING & CARING FOR SELF	60
DON'T EVER BE ASHAMED OF THE SCARS	61
MY SELF-CARE JOURNAL NOTES	62

ALWAYS VALIDATE YOURSELF!

Adrienne K. Thomas (Author)

†

"But what things were gain to me, these I have counted loss for Christ. Yet indeed I also count all things loss for the excellence of the knowledge of Christ Jesus my Lord, for whom I have suffered the loss of all things, and count them as rubbish, that I may gain Christ." Philippians 3: 7-8 NKJV

INTRODUCTION

I started focusing more on writing in 2009 to help me through a rough patch in my personal life. I had experienced some things that made me question myself, my work, and my relationship at the time. I was no longer hopeful or prayerful. I refused outside help and I turned away from listening to God. I was at my weakest point. I did not know who I was anymore. I was so worried about how I would make it and how my children would react to whatever was about to take place.

During these trying times, I was working in the mental health field where I had to give a listening ear and support parents/caregivers on decisions they often had to make for themselves and/or their child(ren). Looking back on that time, I had no idea how I had the energy to give hope, encourage, uplift, and inspire others but never did any soul-searching for myself of how to support my situation and stay prayerful through it all.

After days of being at my lowest point, I decided to take some time for myself. One evening, after my kids were asleep, I was flipping through the TV and found myself watching a church program. A minister was talking about meditation. After listening to the program, I decided to follow through by finding a small place in my home to cry out to God and ask Him for help. During my time of silence, through tears, in my darkest and weakest moment, I felt God's presence telling me to *hold on and to keep fighting.*

The next day, when I woke up, I knew God was speaking to me, but I didn't know where to start. I was in a toxic storm. I felt I had lost out on everything I had worked towards and I didn't know how to fix it. I had read a story recently in Our Daily Bread called *Hope.* After reading it, I found myself praying more.

During this time, the relationship I was in was not going well. I began to believe I was dragging this person into a situation he did not want to be in, which I felt was going to end up hurting me even more. It was stalling the plan I wanted for my future, which included having peace, happiness, and taking care of my children. I found myself asking God why I had to be re-hurt and disappointed when this other person made the decision about where they wanted to be. I had no fight or strength left. I was tired of crying and mentally fighting. I asked myself why and how I had allowed this to happen. I was living behind a mask in my relationship nightmare. I was pouring into everyone else's cup but my own cup was empty. YES, my own cup was empty. The person who felt she had it all together and had found someone that was true about their word. However, in the relationship I began to see red flags including infidelity, lack of love, mistrust, and no respect for home. My kids watched all of this but were too young to fully understand. I shielded a lot from them because of my lack of strength to speak up. I found myself sinking into depression until I was mentally broken. I prayed for God to give me my spirit and my mind back–He did.

We all have struggles in life. Many of us deal with learning how to love ourselves first, and allow our boundaries to go out the window. When things start to make us unhappy, many times we smile through it just to make everyone else happy. The way we allow others to break us down during times we need support the most can lead us to a dark place. This is not a good place to be.

Nevertheless, this book is not so much about my past relationship but rather a trigger that showed me I was lacking self-love, self-care, and self-respect. I had lost myself because of how I allowed someone else to treat me. I learned before committing to another person, it is important to have a mutual understanding that the two of you are not in things alone, but together. We must have enough faith and believe that God is FIRST. He is the only one who can redirect and rebuild us.

I am excited to have this workable journal come to life. Inside these pages it is my hope that you will find inspiration, positive affirmations, messages, and fun interactive activities that will make you think about who you really are and challenge you to learn how well you know YOURSELF.

I am thankful for being able to share this and to tell you that life isn't always a walk in the park. It takes lots of self-encouragement, positive self-talk, and prayers to change whatever you're struggling with whether it is mental, physical, emotional, spiritual or financial.

Always remember, there is light at the end of the tunnel. Whatever you lose in life you will either gain it back, if it is meant to be, or it might be gone forever. If it is gone forever then something better is coming.

I hope this workable journal is a blessing to your life and that it will encourage you to begin to start filling your cup more, starting with SELF.

Adrienne

GAINING THROUGH LOSING

I asked God for strength, that I might achieve,
I was made weak, that I might learn to humbly obey

I asked for health, that I might do greater things,
I was given infirmity, that I might do better things

I asked for riches, that I might be happy,
I was given poverty, that I might be wise

I asked for power, that I might have the praise of men,
I was given weakness, that I might feel the need of God.

I asked for all things, that I might enjoy life,
I got nothing that I asked for, but everything I had hoped for

Almost despite myself,
My unspoken prayers were answered

I am among all men, most richly blessed.

(The Prayer of an Unknown Soldier)

What is Self-Care?

The act of taking care of your mental, physical, and emotional well-being

Self-care has been defined as the process of taking care of oneself with behaviors that promote health and active management of illness when it occurs. Individuals engage in some form of self-care daily with food choices, exercise, sleep, and dental care.

Self-care is the practice of individuals looking after their own health using the knowledge and information available to them. It is a decision-making process that empowers individuals to look after their own health efficiently and conveniently, in collaboration with health and social care professionals as needed.

What is your idea of self-care?

_____

_____

_____

_____

_____

Do you practice self-care on a regular basis? Why or Why not.

_____

_____

_____

_____

WHY IS SELF-CARE IMPORTANT?

Self-care can help reduce stress and enhance your quality of life.

Self-care can help you manage the daily stresses in your life such as academic pressures, tricky relationships, and an uncertain future.

Why is self-care important to you?

_____
_____
_____
_____
_____
_____
_____
_____
_____
_____

THE AREAS OF SELF-CARE

There are **8** main areas of SELF-CARE: physical, psychological, emotional, social, professional, environmental, spiritual, and financial.

✓ **Physical self-care can include:**

Movement of the body, nutrition, health, sleep, and resting needs.

Examples of physical self-care:

- Dancing
- Watching a good movie
- Getting enough sleep (7-9 hours per night)
- Eating nourishing foods

What are some of your physical self-care practices?

_____
_____
_____
_____
_____
_____
_____

✓ **Psychological self-care includes:**

Learning new things, practicing mindfulness and creativity.

Examples of psychological self-care:

- Practicing mindfulness
- Detoxing
- Learning a new skill
- Surfing the internet

What are some of your psychological self-care practices?

_____
_____
_____
_____
_____
_____
_____

✓ **Emotional self-care includes:**

Enhancing emotional literacy, navigating emotions, increasing empathy and managing stress effectively.

Examples of emotional self-care:
- Making time for reflecting on feelings
- Saying *no*
- Practicing self-compassion
- Being aware of your emotional boundaries

What are some of your emotional self-care routines?

_____
_____
_____
_____
_____
_____
_____

✓ **Social self-care means:**

Having a supportive group and network of relationships around you that you can trust and turn to.

Examples of social self-care practices:

- Keeping your commitments to other people
- Asking for help when you need it
- Meeting new people
- Spending time with family and friends

What are some of your social self-care practices?

_____
_____
_____
_____
_____
_____
_____

✓ Professional self-care includes:

Sharing your strengths and gifts, living your purpose and having clear professional boundaries.

Examples of professional self-care:

- Eating a nourishing lunch/meal each day
- Decluttering your work environment
- Having clear professional boundaries
- Participating in professional development opportunities

What are some of your professional self-care practices?

_____
_____
_____
_____

_____
_____
_____

✓ Environmental self-care means:

Having an organized, well maintained and clutter-free work, business, and home environment. Having clean clothes and a well-maintained mode of transportation.

Examples of environmental self-care:
- Decluttering your home environment
- Monitoring technology time
- Cleaning the kitchen after a meal
- Maintaining a clean and safe living environment

What are some of your environmental self-care routines?

_____
_____
_____
_____
_____
_____
_____

✓ Spiritual self-care means:

Having beliefs and values that are important to you and guide your life.

Some examples of spiritual self-care:
- Meditating
- Reflecting in a journal
- Going on a retreat
- Nature walking

What are some of your spiritual self-care routines?

_____
_____
_____
_____
_____
_____
_____

✓ Financial self-care

Being responsible with your finances and having a conscious relationship with money.

Examples of financial self-care:
- Knowing where your income is coming in
- Knowing where your expenses are due and paying them on time
- Completing your tax responsibilities on time
- Spending and saving money wisely

What are some of your financial self-care practices?

_____
_____
_____
_____
_____
_____

WHO AM I?

Do you realize YOU do not need anyone except SELF? YOU are self-sufficient because YOU and only YOU must be responsible for your own happiness. Learn how to trust the strength of your own heart. Know that YOU can make your own happiness even when things get difficult.

Answer the following questions.

How well do you know yourself? (Explain)

_____
_____

How old do people think you are? (Explain)

_____
_____

How old do you feel? (Explain)

_____
_____

What is a nickname for you? (Explain)

_____
_____

What is your personality like?

_____
_____
_____
_____

What are some of your likes?

What are some of your dislikes?

What is your love life like?

Write a short summary about yourself.

SELF-CARE QUIZ

Take the following Self-Care Quiz
(Check True or False) Be honest.

I eat healthy most days.	☐ TRUE	☐ FALSE
I rarely eat fast foods.	☐ TRUE	☐ FALSE
Most of the time I am not stressed.	☐ TRUE	☐ FALSE
I can say 'no' without feeling bad/guilty.	☐ TRUE	☐ FALSE
I exercise at least 1 or 2 times per week.	☐ TRUE	☐ FALSE
I am productive and concentrate well at work.	☐ TRUE	☐ FALSE
I spend time on things I love to do.	☐ TRUE	☐ FALSE

I feel energized and well rested most of the time.	☐ TRUE	☐ FALSE
I do not feel like I need to be perfect.	☐ TRUE	☐ FALSE
I am worthy and deserving of love	☐ TRUE	☐ FALSE
I believe I am special	☐ TRUE	☐ FALSE
I have a purpose for living.	☐ TRUE	☐ FALSE
I am able to communicate my needs/wants.	☐ TRUE	☐ FALSE
I am accepting and loving of my body.	☐ TRUE	☐ FALSE
I need to be in a romantic relationship to feel whole.	☐ TRUE	☐ FALSE
It is okay to make mistakes and not be the best	☐ TRUE	☐ FALSE
My feelings matter.	☐ TRUE	☐ FALSE
I place equal importance on my feelings as I do on other people's feelings.	☐ TRUE	☐ FALSE
I deserve good things in my life.	☐ TRUE	☐ FALSE

After taking the Self-care quiz did you find out if you are practicing self-care? If so, how does this make you feel? If you are not practicing self-care, did taking this quiz make you want to start practicing self-care? Why or Why not?

_____

_____

_____

_____

_____

_____

_____

_____

_____

SELF-CARE QUIZ RESULTS:

Give yourself a "0" for each TRUE response. Give yourself a "1" for each FALSE response. Add up your points to reveal total points scored.

0-3 points – you have healthy self-care routine. Taking this quiz will reinforce what you need to do to maintain it and provide you with new tools and resources.

3-6 points– you could use some help with improving your self-care routine and being available for yourself before you start to become overwhelmed. Taking this quiz can guide you to making necessary changes.

+6 points– your life is out of control. Act now to being making yourself a priority.

YOUR SELF-WORTH

MYTH OR FACT?

Read the definitions below about myth versus fact, then look at the statements and check the appropriate box whether you think the statement is a myth or fact.

Myth/miTH/ -*noun*

A traditional story, especially one concerning the early history of a people or explaining some natural or social phenomenon, and typically involving supernatural beings or events. (2) A widely held but false belief or idea.

Fact /fakt/- *noun*

A thing that is known or proved to be true. (2) Information used as evidence or as part of a report or news article. (3) The truth about events as opposed to interpretation.

It is impossible to have self-worth and not be selfish.	Myth ☐ Fact ☐
I shall love others more than I love myself.	Myth ☐ Fact ☐
Other people are more important than I am.	Myth ☐ Fact ☐
I must help others before I help myself.	Myth ☐ Fact ☐
Other people have influence over myself worth	Myth ☐ Fact ☐
Pleasing others is the most important thing to be worthy.	Myth ☐ Fact ☐
Self-worth comes from what others think about me.	Myth ☐ Fact ☐

SELF-CARE MENU

We all need food to survive, but we need mental food too. When life became busy for me, I would lack eating a physical and mental health meal. I now take the time to eat at least 2-3 meals a day for my physical as well as mental needs. I enjoy watching TV, bowling, spa treatment, meditation, lighting a good smelling candle and writing in my journal. I suggest you take the time to enjoy a physical daily meal by taking time for breakfast, lunch, and dinner. Take at least a mental meal monthly. Gradually increase it to weekly then daily. We must take care of ourselves.

Appetizers
- Take a break
- Deep breathing
- Listen to music
- _____
- _____
- _____

Beverages
- Drink your water
- Have a cup of tea
- Fancy coffee
- _____
- _____
- _____

Specials
- Call a friend or family
- Practice yoga
- Engage in a hobby
- _____
- _____
- _____

Entrees
- 8 hours of sleep
- Movie and snack
- Focus on letting go
- _____
- _____
- _____

Sides
- Write in journal
- Do some exercises
- Go for a bike or car ride
- _____
- _____
- _____

Desserts
- Take a long bath
- Light a candle
- Pamper your body
- _____
- _____
- _____

HOW DOES LOVE DEFINE YOU?

Love - an intense feeling of deep affection; a great interest and pleasure in something. (Feel deep affection for someone)

To figure out if I found true love, it was important for me to first understand what true love entailed. Essentially, true love means that you have an unwavering, unbreakable, and unparalleled fondness and devotion for your partner. It is also defined by an emotional as well as physical connection with the other person that runs immeasurably deep.

What you Should Know: Learn to leave your struggles behind and live a life full of love, laughter, and joy.

What are some things you no longer struggle with?

_____

_____

_____

_____

What is your work-through plan to start the process of overcoming things you are still struggling with?

_____

_____

_____

_____

What are some ways you find contentment?

_____

_____

_____

_____

GRATEFUL

GRATEFUL: "Feeling or showing an appreciation of kindness; thankful."

There were times of uncertainty when I started to realize how powerless I was when trying to control my own destiny. I wanted to stop remembering the bad, but it was hard to turn that side of my brain off.

Think of the worst times in your life. Think of your sorrows, your losses, your sadness and then remember that here you are, able to remember them. You made it through the worst times of your life. You got through the trauma, you got through the trial, you endured the temptation, you survived the bad relationship, and you are making your way out of the darkness.

What You Should Know: Take time to look and see where you are now. When times are good, learn not to take prosperity for granted. Practice being grateful on a daily basis by recognizing the things you are grateful for on a daily basis.

Complete the following:

I am GRATEFUL for my family because:

_____
_____
_____
_____
_____

I am GRATEFUL for who I am because:

_____
_____
_____
_____
_____

I am GRATEFUL for my relationships and friendships because:

_____
_____
_____
_____
_____

I am GRATEFUL for my career/job because:

_____
_____
_____
_____
_____

List some of the things that have occurred in your life today, this week, and this month for which you are GRATEFUL:

Today
_____
_____

This Week
_____
_____

This Month
_____
_____

MEDITATION

Meditation: "the action or practice of meditating; a written or spoken discourse expressing considered thoughts on a subject."

When I initially heard about meditation I said to myself I would never need to practice meditation. I felt it was because God knew me and knew what I was going through, and I could handle it. As time went on, however, I started feeling hopeless, worried, broken, and depressed. One lonely weekend I was watching TV, flipping through the guide when I saw a title by a minister called "The Importance of Practicing Meditation." I selected to watch it. The minister said, "We all make time with family and friends but what about making time with God?" I found spiritual and focused meditation was the right meditation for me.

Meditation
1. Mindfulness – No teacher to guide you do alone
2. Spiritual – Home/Worship, silent and seek spiritual growth.
3. Focused – Anyone who needs additional focus in their life.
4. Movement – Peace in action and prefer to let their minds wander
5. Mantra – Chanting loudly or quietly turning in your environment.
6. Transcendental – Structure maintaining meditation practice.

Meditating on these requires different mindsets. Which meditation do you feel is right for you? Why?

_____
_____

Here Are Some Ideas For Using Your Words EVERYDAY.
- Meditate on one word a day
- Be mindful of the day's word as you go about your daily life
- You will see these words in some inspirational quotes

- Research each word to see how inspirational they can be
- Encourage someone by sharing an inspirational word

Do you or have you practiced meditation? If so, what did you find some of the benefits to be?

_____
_____
_____
_____
_____
_____
_____
_____

Make your own list below of everyday words you might want to use and reflect on when you go into meditation.

_____
_____
_____
_____
_____
_____
_____
_____
_____
_____
_____

BROKEN

Broken: having been fractured or damaged and no longer in one piece or in working order; (of a person) having given up all hope; despairing.

What You Should Know: The relationship I was in hurt me to the point that I felt like everything was tainted. This was a response to being hurt so badly that I believed the only way to protect myself from more pain was to emotionally detach from everyone and everything. Nothing could hurt me because nothing mattered like this pain. I built walls around it and isolated myself to the point that anger and rage festered inside of me. As I began praying and reading, I learned that these feelings, due to not wanting to build up another disappointment, would rob me of my ability to enjoy life and relationships. It was easier to pass on anything potentially enjoyable because I believed it might turn painful. Love, hope, trust, loyalty became lies. I speak from my own experience. You do not want what I felt, which was broken and empty.

Life is not ALWAYS perfect ....

The problem you are facing is not the end of the world!

It can be a new and different start of life

Pencil still writes

FAILURE

Failure: lack of success; the omission of expected or required action

What You Should Know: Failure is not falling down but refusing to get up. I had lack of persistence. I did not realize that more people fail, not because they lack knowledge, but because they quit. I learned two important words: *persistence* and *resistance*. Persist in what must be done and resist what ought not to be done. Try new approaches and goals. Persistence is important, but repeating the same actions repeatedly, hoping that this time you'll succeed, probably won't get you any closer to your objective. I had to look at my previous unsuccessful efforts and decide what to change. My advice is to keep adjusting, make corrections, and use your experience as a guide.

My Goals	How to reach my goals

A SPECIAL WORD ABOUT MOTHERS

Mothers are the strongest and most resilient human beings in the world. They know how to masquerade their feelings. Most of the time the world will not notice when a mother is sad or sometimes even suffocated. You might be surprised how many times a mother cries while sitting in her car or in the bath/shower. Sometimes she may cry while cleaning the house or folding laundry. She may cry, simply out of feeling powerlessness or because of extreme tiredness that sometimes surrounds mothers who give everything to make their family and loved ones happy. Mothers might cry alone because they do not want anyone to pity their tears. However, whenever she shows her face again, she looks normal. She will try to give her children and family the best face and a big smile as if everything is fine.

What You Should Know. Mothers, should seek help and have a support team they can confidently confide in during times of stress, problems, or when she is just plain tired from the cares of the world and all the duties and responsibilities she faces on a daily basis as a mother.

DO NOT BE AFRAID TO ASK FOR... HELP!

Who is on your self-care team?

Who can help you when you are feeling down?

Who can you wake up at any time of the night?

Who will not judge you?

FORGIVE

Forgive: To stop feeling angry or resentful toward (someone) for an offense, flaw, or mistake.

I was having a hard time going through life. I did not understand why I had to forgive those who had wronged me. I found myself soaking in hurt and disappointment. I went to church one Sunday. The pastor was preaching about forgiveness. She said, "If you're wondering how to overcome things then learn how to forgive." I broke down in tears because I felt that I had done everything I needed to do in my relationship, only it still wasn't good enough for the other person. I could not understand why I needed to forgive the other person when I had done nothing wrong. My heart was heavy. I wasn't prepared to forgive that person at the time. I thank God for staying on me, for softening my heart so I could forgive the other person. When I forgave, I felt much better for having done so.

What You Should Know: I learned that forgiveness is for *self* and not the other person. Jesus forgave everyone for things He didn't do wrong. You might not ever forget but at least find the strength to FORGIVE.

Complete the following (be detailed).

I remind myself to:

_____

_____

_____

Today I forgive myself for:

_____

_____

To move on I acknowledge that I was wrong in how I:

I deserve forgiveness because:

The next time I am faced with a similar decision I will:

I should forgive others because:

ARE YOU AN OVERCOMER?

Overcomer: A person who overcomes something; one who succeeds in dealing with or gaining control of some problem or difficulty.

What You Should Know: We all face situations, problems, encounters and other events that we may need to overcome in life. Some situations we face may be more difficult than others for us to overcome. I encourage you to never give up when you face difficulties and problems. Instead, learn how to pray and stay focused on your goals. Try to ignore the distractions that come along and keep believing that you can overcome whatever is causing your problems.

Answer the following questions. Be honest and detailed.

What are some things you need to overcome or have already overcome?

_____
_____
_____
_____
_____
_____

What are some of your strengths, gifts, and talents?

_____
_____
_____
_____

What motivates you to keep going?

How do you meditate?

What are some of the hardest lessons you have learned?

What are some of your proudest moments?

___

Make a list of positive messages that you will give or learn to give to yourself.

___

MY FUTURE

We all have dreams, goals, and desires that we want to fulfill in life. Imagine your life in the next one year, five years and 10 years. Include any of your hopes and dreams, how you would like your life to look, and describe how you will accomplish these things.

In 1 year I hope to:

_____

_____

_____

_____

_____

_____

_____

_____

_____

5 years I hope I am:

_____

_____

_____

10 years I want my life to look like this:

HEALTHY RELATIONSHIP CHECKLIST

When learning self-love, it is important to take time to evaluate the various aspects of your key relationships. You can go many years in relationships allowing the status quo to exist. You should reflect inward and pay attention to trust, communication, and patterns of self-doubt.

What You Should Know: Learn ways to identify red flags. They may signal a conflict with your ability to love yourself by neglecting to notice or address balance, power, and control or a lack of mutual trust or respect in a relationship. This could cause unhealthy patterns. These red flag behaviors can begin to chip away at your self-esteem and potentially lead to a never-ending cycle of unhealthy relationship dynamics. Harmful, toxic relationships can breed under barren conditions where self-love fails to take root and grow. Time spent addressing these issues can serve as the springboard for a positive life-changing transformation.

Check to see if any of the dynamics below are present in your relationships. Address these red flag issues accordingly to assure a healthy relationship can or does exist.

- ☐ Coercion
- ☐ Controlling behavior
- ☐ Gaslighting
- ☐ Invisibility
- ☐ Jealousy
- ☐ Mistreatment
- ☐ Name calling
- ☐ Threats

What are some other red flags for you?

_____

_____

_____

SELF-CARE ACTIVITIES

Are You Practicing Self-Care and Staying Healthy

- Being active and workout on a regular basis is recommended for physical health
- Exercise produces mood-stabilizing
- Going on short daily walks can help your overall mood, plus fresh air!
- Riding a bike, playing a sport
- Drinking water & eating well fruit and vegetables
- Getting enough good sleep at least 8 hours
- Planning ahead and creating a routine
- Asking for help

On the following pages are some fun ideas, games, puzzles, and projects to help you with practicing and/or learning self-love and self-care.

VISION BOARD ACTIVITY

Let's have some fun making a vision board!

A <u>vision board</u> is a collage of images and words that you should display in a prominent place to remind you WHY you do what you do every day. Use images and words that spark your motivation and remind you of your values, goals, beliefs, and/or dreams. Your vision board can also be filled with things that inspire you or leave you feeling happy.

Listed below are some questions that may help spark mental images for your vision board:

Vision Board Activity Ideas

- What are my strengths?
- What are my short-term goals?
- What are my long-term goals?
- Who matters most to me?
- What do I like to do for fun?
- What new activities am I interested in or willing to try?
- What are my values?
- What do I believe in?
- If I could have one wish, what would it be?
- Where do I feel safest?
- What or who gives me comfort?
- If I wasn't afraid, I would do what?
- What is my proudest accomplishment?
- Am I a night owl or an early bird?
- What do I like about my job/career?
- What do I do to show self-love and self-care?
- What am I passionate about?
- What is my happiest memory?
- What do my dreams tell me?
- What is my favorite book? Movie? Band?
- What is my favorite Color? Animal?
- What am I grateful for?
- What do I like to do when I am feeling down?

Items you will need for your vision board.

Vision Board Essentials

- ✓ Stick Glue (highly recommended) or Tape
- ✓ Magazines,
- ✓ Books with pictures, letters, words, etc.
- ✓ Scissors
- ✓ Markers, crayons, colored pencils
- ✓ Stickers
- ✓ Jewels, glitter
- ✓ Personal pictures
- ✓ Any and/all items you want to include

MY VISION BOARD

Tape or stick glue your Vision Board items below:

MY VISION BOARD

Tape or stick glue your Vision Board items below:

VISION BOARD ACTIVITY QUESTIONAIRE

What did you enjoy most about the Vision Board activity?

___

Where did you display your Vision Board?

___

When do you reflect on your Vision Board?

___

How do you feel when you look back at your Vision Board?

___

SMALL STEPS TOWARDS A MORE POSITIVE APPROACH
Puzzle #1

```
I J S J T H M N O I T A V I T O M L N G
L K K R K I S M A C J Y Y N R E U R A
Z S A X N Y D P A F Z X C G Y F F F H C
I T G D F C G U B F A I E N S L K R X F
S X F A V C F V C Z B I R K G O R E P V
W U P I K R H H R K V P H Q J V J W I A
L S H Q B C H Q V N U M L T C E T O D V
W Q T U Q P N D O D F Y Z N Q N S P G T
E L F N M S F R M N I O R C E E O H Z D
R C U W C S F E W C L O Y M M Z Y E U K
W M A K K W F Z K H F N E M I F O F Y O
I L H E P R O K D D Z G I G R I M K P K
T U A B P B H U L K A L K H R Z W C M U
R N M D Y I H N P R G C D I D E Q A Y N
A K X L O X J A U S P D G U N P A C D P
N X I K D P Z O H E R G N G U D B Z T K
C I C L S V C D C L I S Q H I C N B H W
Q A J R D N E X C I T E M E N T Z E J E
B D C X E A C O F S O S U Z B E C F S Z
Z Z Q N I V D I T Z T Q W H W B J Z E S
```

Find the following words in the above puzzle:

Encouragement	Excitement	Kindness
Love	Mindful	Motivation
Peace	Powerful	Start

Puzzle #2

```
G V Y C R T H V H Y A R J H J J D A D S
V N A L X U U M J A W W W V T M S F B U
V W I L E O R Y Y O A I L M A T S P H F
U I S T U Y U A A Y R L X Z E M E Z L M
I V I L A A T F F W E Z W R F C L X O F
G C J T A N B Q L Y N C U J J W T V O M
F B A U G B I L T Y E S D S G I I U D Z
A J M L W L Q C E Q S N C K R S M V N A
K B J G V E L N S A S Z T T C D I Q I G
D E O C L H G F E A N B K I K O L W X D
H G U Y N B B R D H F S T W N M I R M R
K Y X C G R Q S J M F W W R S U R J A H
Z L W Z E G A W I B P C Q X X F N Q B B
C K J A M C F Z I W D V F E U B B H X F
W M T E T A N O I S S A P M O C C X D L
V H J S F K N Z B R H I E V B N L K M O
E Q S V U K Y T G L V L F O J P I E X S
X K Y T X V B L Q M K H B C Z A P E G T
I N R O G Z I B J E S T H A Y C Q D E B
P F R P N D B S Z Z V T B W G C S O U L
```

Find the following words in the above puzzle:

Awareness	Breathe	Compassionate
Fascinating	Limitless	Reassure
Soul	Valuable	Wisdom

WHO IS THAT IN THE MIRROR?

Look in the mirror or your phone camera. Draw a picture of yourself or attach a picture to this page below:

Tell yourself you are beautiful inside.
Next, point to yourself and say, "YOU, yes, YOU are beautiful."

God created you in his image. Genesis 1: 27 KJV
Read Psalms 139: 14-16

MONTHLY SELF-CARE ACTIVITY CALENDAR

Take some time for yourself.
Add activities to your calendar and hang it up.

Sunday	Monday	Tuesday	Wednesday	Thursday	Friday	Saturday
Read a good book or magazine	Have a sweet treat	Go for a walk, jog, bike ride, roller skate	Start a journal or write in your journal	Watch a good movie or TV show	Practice Meditation	Chill & enjoy doing nothing

SELF-CARE CALENDAR 1

*Instructions: Here are some things you can practice for self-care.
Add activities to your calendar and hang it up.*

SUNDAY	MONDAY	TUESDAY	WEDNESDAY	THURSDAY	FRIDAY	SATURDAY
MENTALLY PREPARE FOR A GREAT WEEK			½ WAY		TIME TO RECHARGE IT'S THE WEEKEND	
MENTALLY PREPARE FOR A GREAT WEEK			½ WAY		TIME TO RECHARGE IT'S THE WEEKEND	
MENTALLY PREPARE FOR A GREAT WEEK			½ WAY		TIME TO RECHARGE IT'S THE WEEKEND	
MENTALLY PREPARE FOR A GREAT WEEK			½ WAY		TIME TO RECHARGE IT'S THE WEEKEND	
MENTALLY PREPARE FOR A GREAT WEEK			½ WAY		TIME TO RECHARGE IT'S THE WEEKEND	

SELF-CARE CALENDAR 2

Instructions: Here are some things you can practice for self-care. Cut out and glue to your self-care calendar, and hang it up.

BURN OR MELT A NICE CANDLE AND MEDITATE	TAKE A WARM BATH & RELAX	START OR CONTINUE A JOURNAL	DANCE	STRETCH OR DO YOGA
REWARD YOURSELF EAT A SWEET TREAT	TAKE A NAP	GO FOR A JOG, WALK OR RIDE	LISTEN TO MUSIC OR BOOK AUDIO	START OR CONTINUE SOME CRAFTING
DECLUTTER YOUR SPACE	CREATE A 'THANKFUL' LIST	SAY "I LOVE MYSELF"	COOK YOUR FAVORITE MEAL OR DESSERT	GET A MASSAGE
CALL SOMEONE AND TALK ABOUT SELF-CARE	READ YOUR FAVORITE BOOK	DO A BRAIN DUMP	CALL AND CHECK ON A LOVED ONE OR FRIEND	WATCH YOUR FAVORITE MOVIE OR TV SERIES
CREATE A BUCKET LIST	PAINT/DRAW A PICTURE AND FRAME IT	TAKE A WARM BATH & RELAX	SHOULD I SAY 'NO' OR 'YES'	CUT YOUR TIME FROM THE ELECTRONIC WORLD

SELF-CARE CALENDAR 3
CREATE YOUR OWN

Write words, cut out magazine pictures, draw a picture, or add your own ideas and activities and hang it up.

SAY "I LOVE MYSELF"

HAVE FUN – COLOR ME

Did you think spending hours coloring was only a childhood pastime? Think again! The adult coloring book trend has spread nationwide, with countless health benefits of coloring for adults. It's time to pull out the crayons, colored pencils, and markers!

Coloring can help:

REDUCE STRESS AND ANXIETY

Coloring has the ability to relax the fear center of your brain, the amygdala. It induces the same state as meditating by reducing the thoughts of a restless mind. This generates mindfulness and quietness, which allows your mind to get some rest after a long day.

IMPROVE MOTOR SKILLS AND VISION

Coloring goes beyond being a fun activity for relaxation. It requires the two hemispheres of the brain to communicate. While logic helps us stay inside the lines, choosing colors generates a creative thought process.

IMPROVE SLEEP

We know we get a better night's sleep when avoiding engaging with electronics at night, because exposure to the emitted light reduces our levels of the sleep hormone, melatonin. Coloring is a relaxing and electronic-free bedtime ritual that won't disturb your level of melatonin.

IMPROVE FOCUS

Coloring requires you to focus, but not so much that it's stressful. It opens up your frontal lobe, which controls organizing and problem solving, and allows you to put everything else aside and live in the moment, thereby generating focus.

You don't have to be an expert artist to color! If you're looking for an uplifting way to unwind after a stressful day, coloring can surely do the trick. Pick something that you like and color it however you like!

Mistakes are proof that you are trying

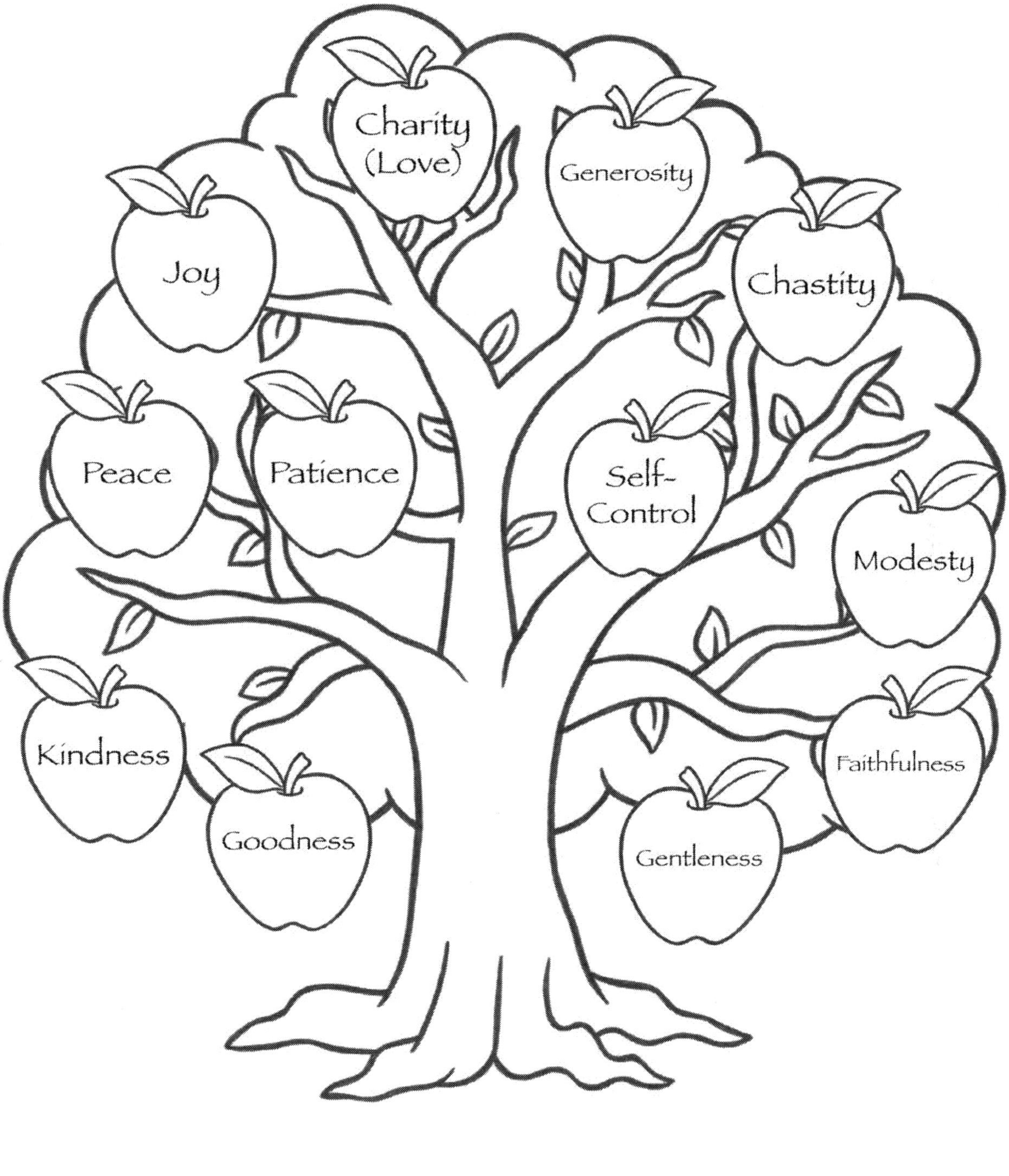
Charity
(Love)
Generosity
Joy
Chastity
Peace
Patience
Self-
Control
Modesty
Kindness
Faithfulness
Goodness
Gentleness

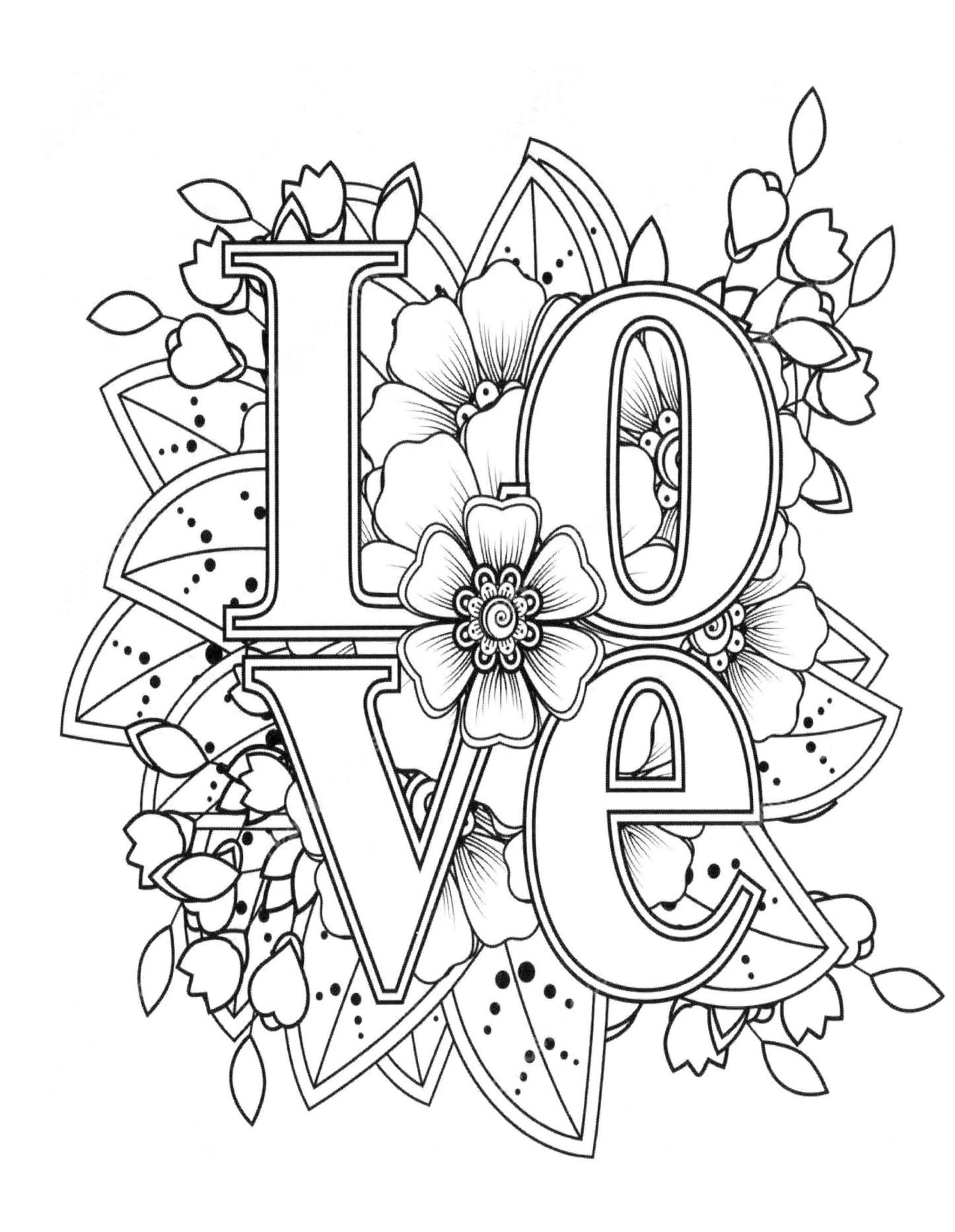

LEARN to let Things you can't control GO

It's OKAY to do what's best for you

NEVER forget who you ARE

Doodle Art Alley ©

I LOVE AND ACCEPT MYSELF AS I AM RIGHT NOW

My dream
My future

BELIEVE IN YOURSELF

DREAM

BELIEVE

ACHIEVE

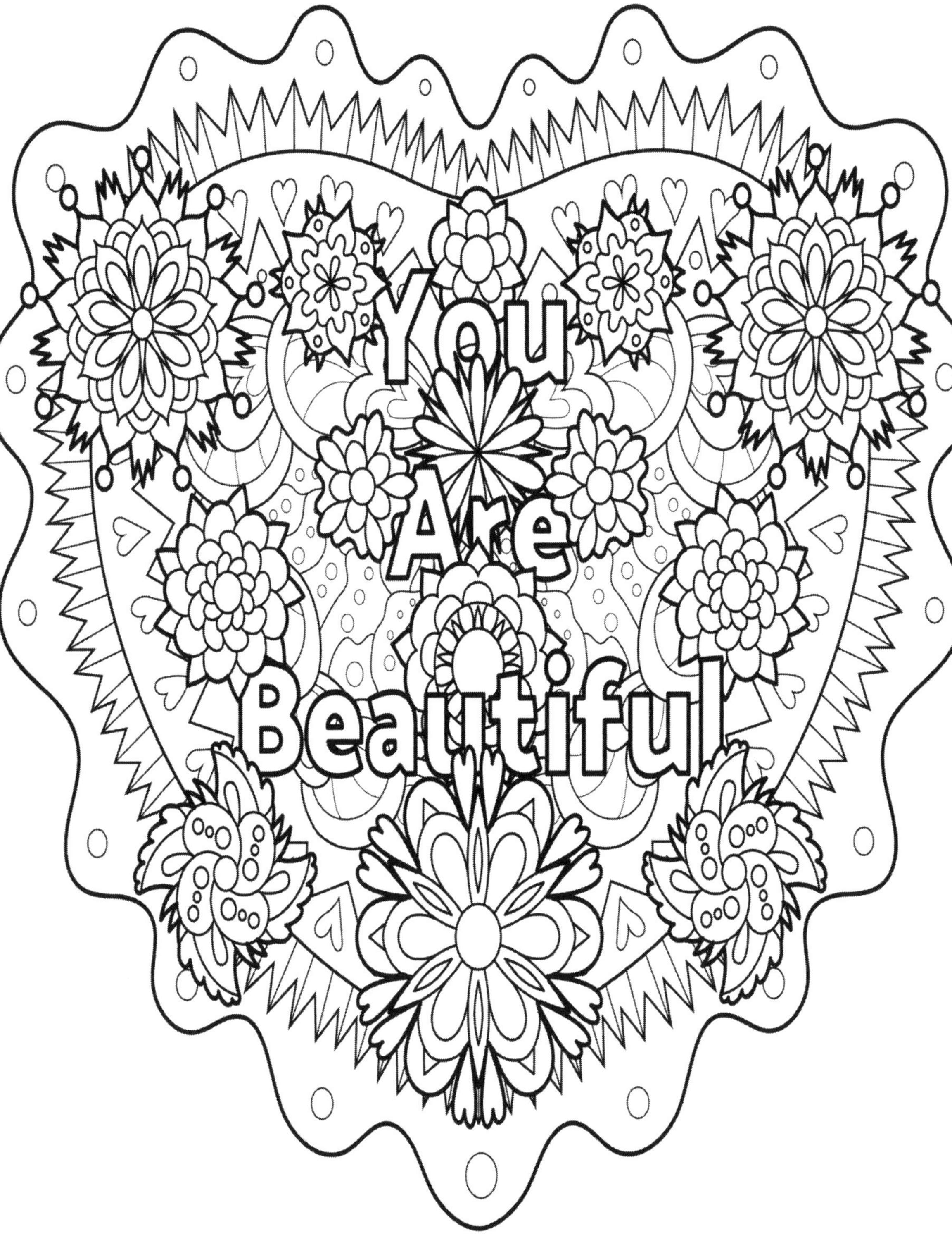
You
Are
Beautiful

make yourself a priority

You deserve the love you keep trying to give everyone else

YOU WERE GIVEN THIS life BECAUSE YOU ARE STRONG enough TO LIVE IT

LOVING & CARING FOR SELF

"Practicing self-love means learning how to trust ourselves, to treat ourselves with respect, and to be kind and affectionate to ourselves."
Brene Brown

In conclusion, loving and caring for self simply means being mindful of your own needs so you are able to support the people you love and care about. Self-care and self-love are requirements for everyone whether young adult, middle age-adult, senior citizen, male or female.

We all juggle through our busy lives which are often filled with school work, careers, families, church, hobbies, and loving and supporting our spouses and children. We all should learn how important it is to devote time for ourselves in order to balance our lives.

When you are not stressed and worried, you can learn how to take better care of yourself physically, mentally, emotionally, and spiritually. Anything that makes you feel better is worth taking a little bit of time out of your day to concentrate on self.

Remember, you cannot fully concentrate or help others if you fail to show yourself self-care and self-love. In order to be productive, it is important to have yourself some *me* time. Without it, you can become overwhelmed and stressed. Being overwhelmed does not make you a bad person, family member, or friend–it makes you human.

My story isn't over...

Adrienne

DON'T EVER BE ASHAMED OF THE SCARS LIFE HAS LEFT YOU WITH

†

A scar means the hurt is over and the wound is closed. It means you conquered the pain, learned the lesson, grew stronger, and moved forward. A scar is the tattoo of a triumph to be proud of. Do not allow your scars to hold you hostage. Don't allow them to make you live your life in fear. You can't make the scars in your life disappear, but you can change the way you see them. You can start seeing your scars as a sign of strength and not pain. *Collectionsofbestquotes.com*

Use the following *Self-care journal* pages to write down your own thoughts and personal feelings. Remember to be true to yourself. You are more than worth it!

MY SELF-CARE JOURNAL NOTES

Available in Paperback from Amazon and other online e-Tailers!
For bulk purchases and autographed copies of this journal,
to arrange speaking engagements, book signings,
special events, and/or conference appearances

CONTACT

Adrienne K. Thomas

atyourblessingresourcelady@gmail.com

Also visit Adrienne's Community Resource Page at:

https://www.facebook.com/groups/680294355684274/

(State of Michigan citizens only)

Made in the USA
Columbia, SC
13 July 2023